Guide Dogs!
A Kids Book About Guide And Other Assistance Dogs

Canine Companions For Independence

By

LIONEL PAXTON

CONTENTS

Introduction: Assistance Dogs	4
What breed of dog?	8
Guide Dogs	11
History of Guide Dogs	11
What do Guide Dogs do	16
Training a Guide Dog	17
Hearing or Signal Dogs	22
What do they do	23
Dogs for Deaf Children	24
Service Dogs	25
Therapy Dogs	26
Companion Dogs	28
Medical Alert Dogs	30
Mobility Assistance Dogs	31
Seizure Response Dogs	32
Psychiatric Service Dogs	34
Assistance Dog Trivia	36
Service Dogs and the Law	41
Dog Health Quiz	44
Quiz Answers	47
Other Books by the Author	51

Independence

I remember the day I met you.

I was captivated by your light
you put your paw into my lap
as if to say everything's going to be alright.

It's truly a match made in heaven.

You seem to know just what I need.

As I take a faltering step,
you now take the lead.

I look to a brand new world
for this is life we travel through.

I can imagine the adventures that await us.

You for me and me for you.

You guide me to higher heights.

And I truly feel a rush
while you give me independence
I give you my trust.

by Nia Green & Ned

Introduction: Assistance Dogs

We have all seen the beautiful Labradors helping blind people walk around the towns, but did you know that dogs can also help deaf people and sick people? A Guide Dog is just one type of Assistance Dog that is trained to help people with an impairment to lead a more independent life.

Dogs can be trained to help people in many ways. They can guide people who are blind, help alert deaf people to sounds; help people in wheelchairs to open and shut doors, press buttons, pick up objects, remove their clothing and even unload the washing machine! Usually a dog is trained for only one of these roles, although in some cases it can be taught to do a combination of roles.

There are 3 groupings of Assistance Dog which are categorized by the specialist nature, capability and aptitude for which the dog is being trained:

- ❖ Guide Dogs support the blind and visually impaired
- ❖ Hearing or Signal Dogs help the deaf and hard of hearing
- ❖ Service Dogs assist and do other work, such as Therapy Dogs, Companion Dogs, Medical Alert Dogs, Mobility Assistance Dogs, Seizure Alert Dogs and Psychiatric Service Dogs

Guide Dogs

Assistance Dogs are dogs which are provided and trained by care organizations to help people with disabilities lead a more independent life. These dogs' help people take charge of their lives in many different ways, giving them independence and reducing their need to rely on others. These animals are protected by law under the Americans with Disabilities Act of 1990 and Americans with Disabilities Amendment Act.

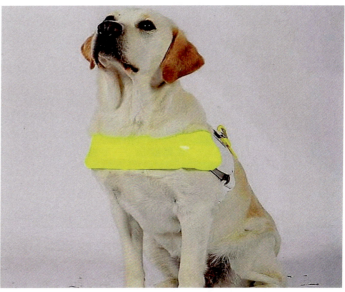

There are numerous Assistance Dog associations world-wide usually registered as charitable organizations. Their aim is to provide Assistance Dogs which are suitably trained and made available to help ensure that people requiring 'assistance' can have the independence which the dog can give. These organizations provide help to thousands of blind and partially sighted people, as well as people with mobility challenges. Their aim is to provide dependable and reliable dogs as well as remove physical and legal obstacles to help people get around on their own. They also campaign passionately for the rights of people with special needs

and visual impairments, and invest millions of dollars into causes such as eye disease research.

Training these dogs to help people takes a long time. For example, it takes about 2 years to train a Guide Dog and match it to a blind person. Many people are involved during this period of training. Assistance Dogs are retired when they are between 8 – 10 years old. When they retire, their owners are given the option to adopt them. If the owner does not want the dog then it is offered to the puppy walker's family, if that's refused then the service looks for a family who wants to adopt a dog. Many retire in their owner's household as a pet whilst being replaced.

There are also other types of special Assistance Dogs such as Working Dogs used by United States Secret Service, Armed and Police Forces. For instance, Navy SEAL Dogs are trained to detect and engage in ways that humans can't. They take part in finding explosives, tracking and guarding people, keeping the enemy busy and much more.

---oooOOOooo---

Funding

Guide Dogs of America does not receive any funding from the Federal, State, or Local Government. They're solely reliant upon donations from individuals, corporations, foundations, chapters and clubs.

If you would like more information on donating your time or money to continue providing guide dogs to blind and visually impaired individuals, visit their Ways to Help page.

What breed of dog?

Assistance Dogs generally come from the breeds which have been classified as working dogs. They include Labradors, German Shepherds, Golden Retrievers, Rottweilers and Collies. A working dog was originally bred to learn and perform tasks to assist or entertain humans. As a result these breeds are easily trained. They also like people love to work, enjoy learning and keeping busy.

Labradors, German Shepherds or Golden Retrievers are the common choice for Guide Dogs. They are chosen for their height so the person can walk with their dog without stooping or bending.

- *Labrador Retriever (or Labrador)*

    This dog was originally bred as a gundog. Its task was to retrieve waterfowl (such as ducks and game birds) which were shot during hunting and shooting parties. The name retriever originated because the dog could retrieve a bird without damaging it. Retrievers enjoy gently holding objects in their mouths - even hands and arms! They also have a good sense of smell which allows them to trace almost any scent and follow the scent until the object is found. These dogs are well natured and are instinctively kind, pleasant, outgoing and controllable. They are also even-tempered and well-behaved around young children and the elderly. All these characteristics make them the most popular breed of dog in the USA as well as the most favored Assistance Dog. Labradors are frequently trained to aid blind and autistic people, act as Therapy Dogs, and perform screening and detection work for law enforcement and other official agencies.

- *German Shepherd*

This breed of dog originated in Germany as early as 1899. It forms part of the Herding Group within the Working Dog classification, because the dog was originally developed to herd sheep. Nowadays, the intelligence, strength, obedience and the ease with which this breed can be trained, results in German Shepherds being the preferred breed for many types of roles, such as Search-and-Rescue, Military and Police roles and even acting. They are the second most popular breed of dog in the USA.

- *Golden Retriever*

Similar to the Labrador, the Golden Retriever was bred as a gun dog to retrieve birds undamaged. This breed instinctively loves water and playing and is easy to train to basic or advanced obedience standards. They are naturally friendly, but their gentle temperament makes them unsuitable for professional guard dogs. However, they are very intelligent, which makes them very adaptable and enables them to fill a number of different roles including acting as a Guide Dog for the blind, Hearing Dog for the deaf, Search-and-Rescue and Detection Dog, Their other characteristics include being very friendly and loyal to their caregivers. Their gentle nature and temperament has led to Golden Retrievers becoming the third most popular family dog breed in the USA.

- *Rottweiler*

The Rottweiler is one of the oldest breeds in the Herding Group. It was used in the mid nineteenth century to herd animals and pull carts full of meat to market. This breed is intelligent, self-confident and adaptable. These characteristics together with a desire to protect make it a suitable bred for an Assistance Dog. Rottweilers are in the top ten most popular dogs in America.

- *Collie*

The Collie is a Working Dog which has a strong herding instinct and has been bred to herd animals. As a result, Collies are very active, agile and easy to train. These dogs are bred to remain calm and relaxed when facing large animals and they must be able to take commands from a trainer. These characteristics, together with the fact that they are naturally friendly, loyal and affectionate and have a gentle temperament, make them an ideal selection for Assistance Dogs.

Guide Dogs

Almost 30 million Americans suffer from vision loss. This number is expected to increase a lot more in the next 10 years, mainly because the average age of the population is increasing. So, care organizations find it challenging to help the growing numbers of people needing help due to either visual disabilities or special needs. The world needs to make sure that as the requirement for Guide Dogs grows, it is organized and equipped to meet these growing needs.

History of Guide Dogs

There is a long history of dogs helping people. The first ever recorded special relationship between a dog and a blind person was painted on a first century mural in the buried ruins of an ancient Roman town called Herculaneum, which was destroyed by volcanic flows in 79 A.D.

Guide Dogs

Historic accounts and records of dogs leading blind people can be found from the Middle Ages in Europe and Asia.

In about 1780, the first organized effort to train dogs to aid blind people started at a hospital for the blind in Paris. Shortly after this, in 1788, Josef Riesinger a blind sieve-maker from Vienna trained a Spitz so well that people often doubted that he was actually blind. Then, in 1819 in Vienna, Herr Johan Wilhelm Klein founded the Institute for the Education of the Blind.

Guide Dogs

The training of modern day Guide Dogs began as late as 1916, when a dog training school was established in Germany with the aim of training dogs to help soldiers who had been blinded during the First World War.

Dorothy Eustis

These students (with their dogs Tartar, left, and Gala) are in the first training class at The Seeing Eye in Nashville, Tenn., in 1929.

Worldwide interest in Guide Dogs was not established until 1927, when American dog breeder Dorothy Harrison Eustis wrote about a German Guide Dog training school. When Dorothy wrote the article, she was already training dogs for the army, police and customs service in Switzerland. Her energy and expertise launched the Guide Dog movement internationally.

Morris Frank, a blind American, heard about this article and wrote to Dorothy Eustis asking her to help introduce Guide Dogs to the United States. When Dorothy received this request, she spent two years training Buddy who was to become America's first Guide Dog. Later Dorothy and Morris established the Seeing Eye School in Morristown New Jersey, which opened in 1929.

The establishment of this school led to news of the use of Guide Dogs spreading internationally. In 1930 the first Guide Dogs were trained in Britain, after two British women contacted Dorothy Eustis. This led, in 1931, to the school, The Guide Dogs for the Blind Association being founded in the UK. The premises are shown above.

Australia's first Guide Dog school was established in Perth in 1951 by blind Doctor Arnold Cook. Doctor Cook brought his first working Guide Dog, Dreena, to Perth in 1950. Dreena was trained in England.

Schools for Guide Dogs have continued to open all around the world. Guide Dogs trained in the schools established by these organizations have helped thousands of disadvantaged people transform their lives. The financial support provided by these organizations and the

commitment of their staff have helped to ensure that the legacy started by Dorothy Eustis continues to this day, giving increased mobility, independence and dignity to blind, partially-sighted and disabled people all over the world.

Guide Dogs

What do Guide Dogs do?

A Guide Dog gives independence and confidence to a partially sighted or totally blind person enabling them to leave their home and get on with their life in the outside world. These dogs are trained to do a number of tasks which are generally taken for granted by people who can see, but make an immeasurable difference to a blind person. The tasks include:

- Walking in a straight line without sniffing the ground
- Stopping at a curb or edge of a road and only crossing when the owner commands
- Walking on the left hand side and a little in front of the owner
- Avoiding branches and other objects located at head height of the owner
- Avoiding narrow spaces where dog and owner cannot fit side by side
- Helping the owner travel on buses and trains
- Helping the owner enter lifts
- Stopping at the bottom and top of stairs
- Lying quietly at the feet of their owner when required.

One of the most important actions a Guide Dog has to do is to stop its owner walking into a dangerous place by refusing to obey a command. For example, the owner may want the dog to move ahead, but there is a large hole, the dog would refuse to obey and would stand still.

An owner gives a dog commands through hand signals and by talking to it. In this way the dog knows what the owner wants the dog to do. As a result, the dogs are trained to watch and listen to their owners.

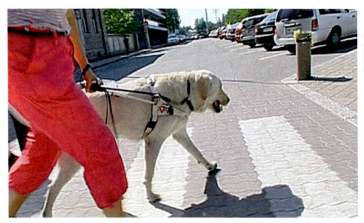

Training a Guide Dog

All Guide Dogs are trained by being rewarded for positive behavior. This means that when the dog does the right thing when commanded, the dog receives a doggy treat and a pat.

It takes two years to train a Guide Dog. The dog goes through the following three distinct stages in the training:

- Puppy raising for the first 18 months
- Dog training with a specialized trainer for five months
- Specialized training with the dog and the blind person for a month to ensure they understand each other and work together as a team.

- *Puppy raising*

Guide Dog training starts when a puppy is given to a family to be looked after. The family will often have school age children. This helps the puppy get used to people of all ages. The puppy remains with the family until it is 18 months old ages.

During the 18 months, the family will house train the puppy to go to the toilet outside and give obedience training to teach the puppy to sit, stay and walk on a lead. The puppy will be taken to the park and on walks to noisy places such as shopping centers and busy areas of a city to help it become accustomed to all sorts of people, noises and places. This will also help the puppy to know a number of the different sounds it will hear when working with a blind owner.
.

- *Dog training*

When the dog is 18 months old, it leaves the puppy training family and is given to a person who will teach the dog to be a Guide Dog. During this time, the dog is trained to walk to commands and avoid obstacles on the footpath such as people, prams, posts and seats. The dog will also be taught to stop when it comes to a road.

The trainers will also train the dog to travel on buses, trams, trains and in cars because it will have to travel on public transport with its owner.

Additionally, the dog is trained to leave enough space between its owner and other people or obstacles to ensure the owner does not collide with an obstacle or another person.

- *Specialized training with the new owner*

In the last stages of the training, a specialized trainer will work with the dog and new owner. This training is to make sure that the dog knows the roads, buses and trains that the owner uses daily. This training will take about one month.

During this time, the owner will learn how the dog thinks and how to care for the dog. Every dog and each owner is unique, so the purpose of this training is to ensure that the dog and owner understand each other and will work well together.

- *What if a dog is not good enough to be a Guide Dog?*

If, during training, it is realized that a dog isn't suitable to be a Guide Dog, it is often trained to be a Companion Dog for a disabled or sick person who could be either a child

or an adult. If the dog still does not suit this, then it can be returned to the puppy raisers as a family dog or given to another family who will have a lovely pet.

Whilst we know intimately the pleasures of companionship and loyalty from our family pet, we don't always fully appreciate the complexity of the relationship, trust and teamwork that develops between a visually impaired person and their Guide Dog. So when developing training programs, careful consideration is taken to ensure that the critical interdependence between the owner and the dog is understood, as well as the unique personalities and traits of each dog and each person, incorporating the circumstances surrounding their lifestyle in order to make a good match.

Hearing or Signal Dogs

These are dogs that are trained and given to people who are deaf or have very little ability to hear. Today organizations are focused on seeking new and better ways of helping this community with innovative methods, whilst keeping abreast of technology advancements.

They dogs let their owners know when sounds, such as the doorbell, telephone, smoke alarms and alarm clock, are being made.

Guide Dogs

These dogs are also useful outside of home because they can let the owner know if someone is calling their name, a vehicle is backing up with an alarm going off or a siren is sounding. Many breeds of dogs are suited for the role of a hearing dog.

- What do they do

    * Wake up a sleeping person when a smoke alarms sounds
    * Let the owner know that a person is at the front door
    * Alert the owner if a kitchen timer is sounding
    * Wake the owner up when an alarm clock goes off.

- *Dogs for deaf children*

Deaf children can feel alone and isolated in their silent world. A hearing dog can help them to go outside and be more like other children. The dog will help them interact with other kids. Kids will want to meet the dog. The dog also helps increase a child's confidence when out of the house or in the backyard. The dog does not go to school with them but stays at home with the parents. Hearing dogs will:

❖ Nudge the child to wake up or pull the covers off the bed when the morning alarm goes off

❖ Let the child know that Mum or Dad is calling

❖ Nudge the child towards a sound.

- *Dogs who do two jobs*

Some people are blind and deaf. Some dogs can be trained to be both the eyes and ears of the person. As well as leading them to the shops and outside of the home, the dog will alert the owner to sounds around the house and when out on walks.

Service Dogs

Service Dogs are not specifically trained to assist people with visual or hearing impairment, but are trained to aid or assist people who are disadvantaged, have disabilities or require special needs. Many are trained by a specific organization whilst others are trained by their handler and at times with the help of a professional trainer.

In order to be selected for training, the dog must pass an entry screening for health and aptitude. This screening takes into consideration the dog's age, size, breed characteristics, physical reliability, trustworthiness of temperament, behavioral history, expected life-span, and anticipated duties. Federal and State laws state that Service Dogs are allowed to go where ever their owner goes. They do not have to wear any specific identifying gear or vests.

There are many amazing jobs that these incredible dogs can be trained to do for adults and children. These generally fall within the following six specialist categories.

Therapy Dogs

There are three different types of Therapy Dogs. The most common type is the Therapeutic Visitation Dog. These are household pets which are taken to visit people in hospitals, nursing, detention and rehabilitation homes to give people something to look forward to. It has been shown that when a dog visits someone this leads to the person visited being brighter and having lifted spirits, they feel better and it's proven to help them in their therapy and treatment after a visit.

 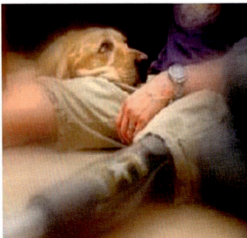 

Animal Assisted Therapy Dogs are the next type of Therapy Dog. These dogs assist physical and occupational therapists in treating recovery patients and can help the patients improve limb movement, regain control, or caring skills.

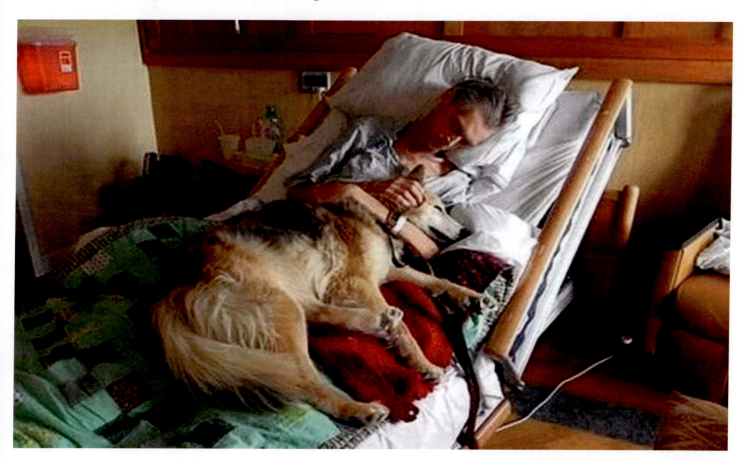

The final type are Facility Therapy Dogs that work in nursing homes, retirement homes, hospices and schools to help people with illnesses such as Alzheimer's disease or other mental illnesses by preventing them from getting into trouble.

- *What do they do*

Therapy Dogs perform a much needed activity for the many people visited by bringing unconditional love and understanding.

These dogs are very friendly and will sit quietly while they are being patted and cuddled. They love meeting and being with people of all ages. While visiting people, they provide affection and comfort to those who are missing their animals at home as it cheers them up to pet another dog. People who have learning difficulties and are in stressful situations

are often visited by dogs, allowing the person to pet and cuddle the dog. This provides a visit which the person really looks forward to. These dogs are:

- Well-tempered
- Well socialized and exposed to many environments and situations
- Affectionate, caring and love to cheer others up!

Companion Dogs

A Companion Dog is trained to be a friend for people who are disabled in a home environment. These dogs can be given to people who have an illness which keeps them indoors and stops them interacting with many other people. Studies show that people with these dogs tend to live longer as a result of leading a life which is healthier and more active. They also feel more fulfilled.

Guide Dogs

- *What do they do*

Companion Dogs can press buttons, pick up objects dropped by their owners, pay for goods in a shop and help their owners around the home in the following ways:

❖ Opening and closing doors, wardrobes and drawers

❖ Removing items of clothing like socks and jumpers

❖ Sounding an emergency bark if their owner is in danger

❖ Offering emotional support, including love and companionship

❖ Assisting in breaking down barriers and reducing social isolation.

They are also taught to dial 911 and can provide an added measure of safety as well as being able to help someone who has difficulty in communicating.

Medical Alert Dogs

These are dogs who are trained to tell if a person is about to be ill. They learn the scent of their owners and how it changes when they become ill. Several breeds of dogs make good Medical Alert Dogs. However gun dogs, such as Labradors, Springer Spaniels, Cocker Spaniels and Retrievers, are the most common breed which are trained to be Medical Alert Dogs.

- ### What do they do

    Medical Alert Dogs communicate with their owners in various ways, like pawing at them, nudging their bodies, arms or legs, jumping up on the owner or barking.

    Some dogs develop their own ways of communicating with their owners, like refusing to let them leave the house or even prevent them standing up. The dogs can press alarm buttons to summons help and are trained to help people in the following situations:

    ❖ Let epileptic sufferers know when they are going to have a seizure or a fit
    ❖ Warn diabetics when their blood sugar is dangerously low or high
    ❖ Warn people with narcolepsy that they are going to fall asleep
    ❖ Recognize severe allergic reactions and get medication to their owner.

Mobility Assistance Dogs

These dogs are trained to help physically disabled people who may be wheelchair-dependent. They help children and adults who suffer from disabilities such as spinal cord injury, brain damage, muscular dystrophy, arthritis, spina bifida, cerebral palsy, and balance problems (Ataxia).

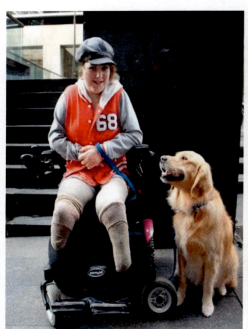 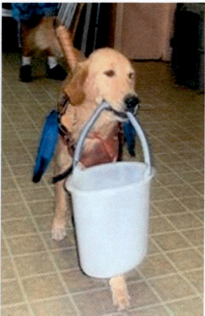 

- What do they do

Mobility Assistance Dogs help their owners decrease dependence on other people and increase their independence, confidence and self-esteem. These dogs are invaluable helpers, quietly serving their owner with tasks that they would find difficult or impossible to do on their own. Some of the tasks which they may help with include:

❖ Assisting with undressing by pulling on clothing
❖ Bringing the phone
❖ Pulling a wheelchair chair up inclines and ramps, and for short distances
❖ Carrying items in a dog backpack
❖ Providing emotional and spiritual support
❖ Offering support by giving the owner a new lease on life.

Seizure Response Dogs

These are dogs that are specifically custom-trained to help those suffering with epilepsy or seizure disorders. They can smell if a seizure is coming on about 30 minutes before and after an attack by responding and acting in a way that is helpful to the person.

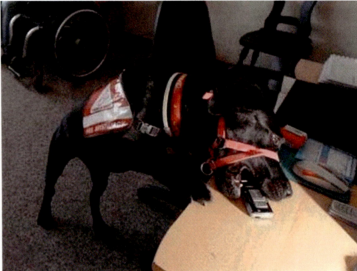

Seizure Response Dogs must be absolutely perfect for the work and specific task, and must be capable of maintaining control in every possible situation. As such only a few organizations are able to provide them.

In addition to performing tasks related to a seizure disorders, these dogs can also be trained to assist with tasks for physical disabilities or hearing loss.

- *What do they do*

    Seizure Response Dogs assist people with tasks such as activating a life-alert system, finding someone to help, retrieving a phone or stimulating a person during a seizure. As a person recovers from a seizure, they are able to get medication, food or act as a brace to help them up and provide comfort. They perform the following tasks:

    ❖ Carry medical alert information and instructions about their owner's medical condition, emergency medication, and oxygen needs

- Summons help by finding another person or activating a medical alert button or pressing a pre-programmed phone
- Move objects away that may possible be dangerous to their owner's body
- Block the path and prevent their owner walking into obstacles, streets, and dangerous areas that can result in bodily injury or death
- Attempt to arouse their unconscious owner during or after a seizure
- Provide the right physical support and emotional support needed.

People with seizure response dogs are often faced with several problems that other service dog handlers typically do not experience. Typically sufferers with these types of conditions do not appear to have anything externally wrong with them. In some cases, the owner is sometimes even reluctant to explain their condition or the dog's trained tasks even in the briefest of terms.

Psychiatric Service Dogs

These dogs are custom-trained to assist their owner's specific needs and have to learn to behave in times of need when in public places and master advanced obedience and public access skills. They are sensitive and able to assist with psychiatric mental disabilities such as post-traumatic stress disorder, Asperger's syndrome, autism, acute anxiety, mood and panic attack, agoraphobia, schizophrenia.

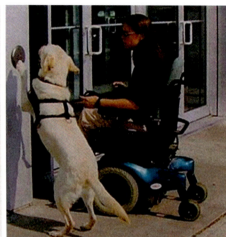

These conditions can be independent or multiple; in some cases several conditions occur together. Regardless of the complexity these dogs can be trained with a host of skills specially developed to support all these conditions. There are specific organizations dedicated to supporting and catering for these dogs and their owners.

- *What do they do*

    Psychiatric Service Dogs are trained to perform tasks which are unique to their owner, and therapeutically work together with the mental challenges. The work and tasks performed by them are directly related to their owner's disability and enhances the lives of their owner. They can

    ❖ Wake their owner for work or school
    ❖ Provide deep pressure for calming effect
    ❖ Provide crowd control and panic prevention in public areas and places

Guide Dogs

- Make sure the surrounding environment is suitable in cases of paranoia or hallucinations
- Assist owner to leave an area by finding an exit
- Answer doorbell, or call 911 on rescue phone, or get or bring help
- Signal and preventative measures like interrupting repetitive or injury prone behavior
- Remind their owner to take their medication
- Fetch or collect objects like mail, phone, clothing or dietary items
- Guide and prevent stressful situations
- Act as a brace if their owner becomes dizzy
- Backpack medical supplies & information
- Offer companionship and emotional support.

Assistance Dog trivia

American philanthropist (person who makes an active effort to promote human welfare) Dorothy Harrison Eustis opened the first US dog training school in New Jersey and called it The Seeing Eye or 'L'Oeil qui Voit' (the name comes from the Old Testament of the Bible; 'the hearing ear and the seeing eye' - Proverbs 10: 12). Her schools in America, Switzerland, and Italy were the first modern era Guide Dog schools that have survived the test of time.

Some people who need an Assistance Dog are allergic to them so there is a breed called a Labradoodle that is used. It is a cross between and Labrador and a Poodle. Poodles don't shed their hair and are better for people with allergies to dogs. Poodles are not normally trained to be Guide Dogs as they don't have the temperament due their highly-strung temperament and the need to be always "on duty" as a working dog.

Guide Dogs

Many countries allow Guide Dogs to go anywhere the public has access to. This means there is no discrimination to people who need an Assistance or Guide Dog.

It is important not to distract a Guide Dog wearing a harness. Always ask a Guide Dog owner before saying hello to their companion.

Two blind people in England are getting married after their dogs met each other and became friends. The dogs are inseparable and their owners have fallen in love too.

One of the benefits of being a Service Dog trainer is that you get to give the animal a happy way of life and you get to help those in our society that are blind, impaired and disabled. You have the opportunity to educate people in your community about Service Dogs and the plethora of things they can do.

Service Dog trainers get to do a lot of good work for the vision-impaired and special needs organizations, and get to spend time working closely with a well-bred dog to do basic

obedience, behavioral and patience routines. They also understand that giving up that dog may be difficult, but know that the dog is going to help someone who really needs it.

Dogs have superior hearing to humans; they are capable of hearing sounds at four times the distance that humans can hear.

Well trained Guide Dogs are intelligent, alert, and always willing to serve and are taught how to deal with traffic, to walk in a straight line in the center of the pavement unless there is an obstacle, not to turn corners unless told to do so, stop at curbs and wait for the command to cross the road, and to determine when it is unsafe to proceed.

Generally, Guide Dogs for the blind are not pets because their purpose is to be working dogs and they have special training that pets do not have. Although they are very much loved by their owners, and they do get to play, much of the time they are working and functioning as they have been trained to lead and protect their owners.

Guide Dog puppies are trained in groups of six to eight dogs. It takes at least 24 months to complete the training.

Guide Dogs

It costs about $8 per day to support each working Guide Dog partnership and a lifetime cost of around $80,000. Each dog is provided free of charge to its owner.

Matching the correct Guide Dog with the correct owner is typically based on the owner's length of stride, height and lifestyle.

When you see a Service Dog in action, they're all business especially when working and you might think that they're always that way, but you'd be wrong, they are trained to know when they are on duty.

Guide Dogs know the difference between on or off duty: as soon as their harness is put on they know they are working and they block out all distractions; when the harness comes off they are as playful and energetic as any other dog

Guide Dogs

To be a puppy walker, you must care for the puppy from when it is between seven to twelve weeks old until it is 14 months old. In that time the puppy is socialized and introduced to situations it will face as a Guide Dog. Puppies then return to the working Guide Dog partnership for six months intensive training and are finally assessed on their personality and temperament traits, health aspects and guiding tasks.

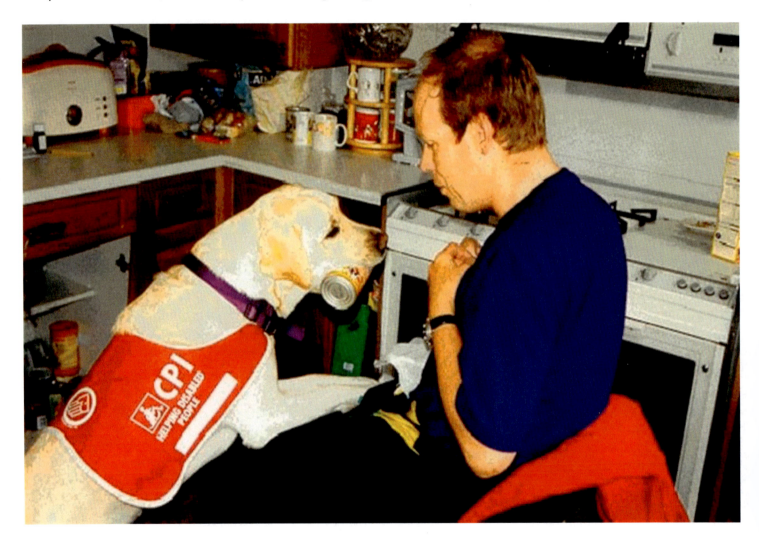

Dogs have a remarkable sense of smell, they are capable of differentiating odors in concentrations nearly 100 million times lower than humans can.

Amazingly Guide Dogs are taught to judge height and width so that their owner does not bump their head, shoulder or body.

Guide Dogs

Male canines are referred to as dogs, females as bitches, dogs younger than a year old as puppies and a group of offspring as a litter.

Guide Dogs are allowed in restaurants with their owners where they sit quietly at their feet. The restaurant owner is not allowed to turn them away.

Service Dogs must be able to go to places where pets are not permitted such as restaurants, office and public buildings, grocery and other stores, even hospitals and doctor's offices.

Exceptional dogs not suitable for guide work are used to help veterans who suffer from Post-Traumatic Stress conditions. They help the veterans gain confidence, start expanding their lives, regain mobility and independence enabling them to re-integrate themselves back into their communities.

To raise a puppy you generally must be at least nine years old and have your parents' permission because it really is a family project. It is good to have other pets because then the pup will become used to other animals and not become distracted by them. You do not have to have had a dog before because you can get all the training you need.

You shouldn't pet a Guide Dog without asking – doing this is like taking the steering wheel away from someone driving a car. This is very dangerous as it puts you, the dog and the blind person at risk because the dog is distracted. The owner may not allow you, not

because they don't like you, but because the Guide Dog only gets praise as a reward for working and if someone else was giving them their reward they may not want to work.

Guide horses are preferred by some people.   A miniature breed of horse is used.   These horses can live a lot longer than a dog, with a expectancy of up to 30 years. Horses have nearly 360 degrees of vision due to their eyes bring on the side of their heads so they are a good alternative to a dog.

Service Dogs and the Law

In the United States, the U.S. Department of Justice, Civil Rights Division, Disability Rights Section applicable law covering Service Animals states that:

"Service animals are defined as dogs that are individually trained to do work or perform tasks for people with disabilities. Examples of such work or tasks include guiding people who are blind, alerting people who are deaf, pulling a wheelchair, alerting and protecting a person who is having a seizure, reminding a person with mental illness to take prescribed medications, calming a person with Post Traumatic Stress Disorder (PTSD) during an anxiety attack, or performing other duties. Service animals are working animals, not pets. The work or task a dog has been trained to provide must be directly related to the person's disability. Dogs whose sole function is to provide comfort or emotional support do not qualify as service animals under the ADA."

Dog health quiz

Have you got what it takes to give your dog a long, healthy life? Test your knowledge and take this popular four minute health quiz now!

- Question 1

    A 20-pound dog should drink about 8 ounces of water every day?

    a. True
    b. False

- Question 2

    Which of these foods is NOT poisonous to dogs?

    a. Grapes/raisins
    b. Avocados
    c. Macadamia nuts
    d. Chocolate
    e. Potatoes
    f. Onions
    g. Garlic.

- Question 3

    If my dog swallows poisonous food, I should make it vomit as soon as possible and call the veterinarian?

    a. True
    b. False

Guide Dogs

- Question 4

About how many dogs and cats aged three or older have tooth and gum disease?

a. 20%
b. 50%
c. 70%
d. 95%

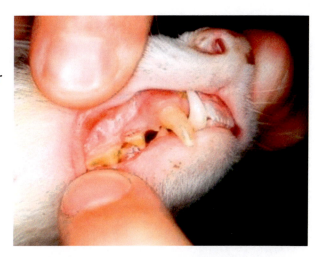

- Question 5

Your dog can live about 15% longer if you look after......?

a. Skin
b. Teeth
c. Nails
d. Bedding

- Question 6

Obesity puts dogs at a higher risk of...?

a. High blood pressure
b. Liver disease
c. Heart disease
d. Diabetes
e. Joint and disc problems
f. Early death
g. All of the above.

- Question 7

    If your dog has fleas, you would know because you would definitely see them on your dog or in your house?

    a. True
    b. False

- Question 8

    Dips and flea collars are NOT a great way to control fleas on your dog?

    a. True
    b. False

Quiz answers

- *Question 1*

    b. False ✓

A 20-pound dog should drink 20 ounces of water every day. The rule of thumb is 1 ounce per pound of pet weight. Easy enough to remember, right?

- *Question 2*

    f. Potatoes ✓

Potatoes are okay for dogs, but all the other human foods listed are dangerous to pets.

- *Question 3*

    b. False ✓

Sometimes you can cause more harm than good by inducing vomiting. Just call your veterinarian as quickly as possible. Or dial the poison control hotline at 1-888-426-4435.

- *Question 4*

    c. 70% ✓

Tooth and gum disease in dogs can lead to lots of problems like pain, tooth decay, diabetes, cancer and more. Regular veterinary checkups can help prevent this.

- *Question 5*

    b. Teeth ✓

Right, dental care. See your veterinarian for a thorough cleaning and pointers on routine dental care and you'll add a year or more to your dog's life!

- *Question 6*

    g. All of the above ✓

Obesity can increase your dog's chances of experiencing any of those problems! Many pet owners don't even realize their dog is obese. Did you know that one out of every four pets is overweight or obese?

- *Question 7*

    b. False ✓

You might see your dog scratch, but it's very possible you will never see a flea, even though they're certainly in your home. Fleas hide in thick or darker fur on dogs. Fleas can cause skin infections, hair loss, tapeworms, anemia and more!

- *Question 8*

    a. True ✓

Forget about dips and flea collars. They don't work that well (never have!), and can be poisonous to pets. These days there are many better options for effective, nontoxic flea control — beginning with the humble flea comb and some soapy water. Talk with your veterinarian about recommended medications to control fleas.

The Guide Dog

There seems to be no way
to describe "Christmas" the dog
without taking a child's wonder
at this blind woman's friend.

With her, "Christmas" the Labrador,
Jan can go many places bravely.
The two clip along at three miles an hour.
That is good walking speed.

What a wonderful help this friendly,
kind dog has been these eleven years.
We give thanks for her service
and companionship.
Good dog "Christmas."

She is loved by Jan, her mistress,
for she is a help and a companion;
good at crossing streets, and walking stairs.
Some animals are special to mankind,
and this is a special dog and friend
for many years.

Soon "Christmas" will retire,
to Carol's house, where she is loved.
Guide Dogs for the Blind
will lead Jan to another canine friend.
What a loss for "Christmas" to go,
but a new friend to come.

by Peter Menkin

Digital Edition V 0.1 – Copyright 2013

All rights reserved. No part of this book may be reproduced by any means whatsoever without the written permission from the authors, except brief portions quoted for purpose of review.

All information in this book has been carefully researched and checked for factual accuracy. However, the authors and publishers make no warranty, expressed or implied, that the information contained herein is appropriate for every individual, situation or purpose, and assume no responsibility for errors or omissions. The reader assumes the risk and full responsibility for all actions, and the authors will not be held responsible for any loss or damage, whether consequential, incidental, special or otherwise that may result from the information presented in this publication.

We have relied on our own experience as well as many different sources for this book, and we have done our best to check facts and to give credit where it is due. In the event that any material is incorrect or has been used without proper permission, please contact us so that the oversight can be corrected.

---oooOOOooo---

Other Books by the Author

Lionel Paxton is an author who has recently turned his hand to children's books. He saw the need for informative picture books for children from the age of 5 to 12. Books are typically the first exposure to learning and art that children get which urges one to make the very best books possible. He understands how important books were to his childhood. With them, he feels as if transported to some parallel universe, a world of grace and wonder.

Navy Seal Dogs by Lionel Paxton

Formats

Kindle Edition

Paperback

Parachute Action Adventure for Kids by Lionel Paxton

Formats

Kindle Edition

Paperback

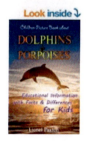

Dolphins and Porpoises Children Picture Book by Lionel Paxton

Formats

Kindle Edition

Paperback

The Legend of the Stars by Lionel Paxton

Formats

Kindle Edition

Paperback

---oooOOOooo---

If you have enjoyed this book, **please** leave a helpful Customer Review on Amazon

---oooOOOooo---

Made in the USA
San Bernardino, CA
20 September 2018